LEADING YOUR

HOA

A 1-Hour Guide to Being a Successful
HOA Board Member

TOM MALETIC

Dedicated to,

Ben, Miles, Jane, Mila and Will

About the Author

Tom Maletic has been active in the HOA industry for the last ten years. He has served as a condominium board member, a board President, and a licensed portfolio community association manager for dozens of communities. He also served as Vice President of Property Management for a management company with over 300 associations and 50 community managers. Tom developed training programs for HOA board members and has written dozens of articles on the key elements and best practices of community association management.

Why I Wrote This Book

I wrote this book to serve as a "primer" on the basics of what you can do to:

- Make your personal time on the board more satisfying
- Produce value for the homeowners in your HOA
- Encourage other homeowners to volunteer to make their HOA a better place to live.

This is a "foundation" book. I want you, as a volunteer board member, to have a foundation of knowledge in what a homeowners association is and how it should work. I have seen too many homeowners associations in which new board members have no basic knowledge in association best practices and they get caught up in the emotions of making decisions for their neighbors. Their volunteer time turns in to a frustrating experience and the existing problems persist with the association.

With a good foundation, I believe you will be able to learn more about community associations and the common issues that confront them. With this book, you will have an outline that will help you organize your thoughts, build on a solid framework and make your volunteer time valuable to you and to your neighbors.

TABLE OF CONTENTS

CHAPTER 1

Volunteering to Help Your Community

Thank you!

Time is one of the most precious commodities in our lives. Dedicating part of your personal time to learning about your homeowners association and collaborating with your neighbors is a very worthwhile endeavor. Thank you for volunteering!

Homeowners associations, or HOA's, can take on many different labels based on their unique physical features and legal conditions. This book is written for all of the various legal types of homeowner organizations, including community associations, town homes, condominiums, common interest developments and homeowner associations.

In my discussions with many new volunteer association board members, perhaps the primary question they have in common is, "I do not know much about homeowners associations. How can I be effective at my board responsibilities?"

The best answer to that question is that you cannot be effective at your role on the board if you do not invest some time in learning how homeowner associations are structured, how they function, and how they can be successful.

Many people who live in a homeowners association believe that their experience as a "homeowner" is the only requirement for being a good board member—that is not the case. Your homeowners association is typically a nonprofit corporation organized under your State's regulations. There are legal implications to everything that a community association—and its board of directors--does and it is imperative that the board members understand the responsibilities and risks involved in the daily operations of the association.

It is important to all of the homeowners that their HOA function effectively. We will go into many of those details throughout this book. But you do not have to "reinvent the wheel" when it comes to operating a successful association. There are thousands of community associations throughout the country—you should learn from their experiences. There are best practices developed by industry associations and professionals for all of the issues and processes that your association will be facing—ask questions of those industry professionals. "How do other associations function?"

Let's start our discussion of your role as a board member with the reason you may have volunteered in the first place. Homeowners volunteer for a number of reasons, including the following,

- A sense of civic duty—some of my neighbors have volunteered, now it's my turn.
- You have a specific skill that is needed by the association.
- You disagree with decisions that have been made—or decisions that are not being made—by the association's current or past boards.
- Or, you just may have self-interest in protecting the substantial financial investment you have made in your home.

Regardless of which reason brought you into the business of the association, it is important that you have a plan for how you will accomplish your objectives during the period of time that you serve on the board.

Imagine that your community association is a railroad passenger train and all of the homeowners are passengers on that train. Each owner gets on and off at different stops during the journey. As a board member you get to be one of the engineers—you need a plan to keep your community train on the right track!

CHAPTER 2

Volunteering for Board Service

Is serving on your HOA board of directors a typical volunteer job?

Volunteering is normally thought of in terms of spending a defined amount of unpaid time helping with a worthy cause—the girl scouts, a local blood bank, breast cancer prevention programs, or parent-teacher-organizations.

Volunteering to serve on your community association board of directors is a "different kind" of volunteering. It is important that you know this. The first difference is that you typically have to be elected to an association board of directors. That means you are offering to volunteer your services and the members of the association have a chance to say "yes or no" to your volunteerism.

Key differences between basic volunteering and volunteering for board service include:

- *Time commitment* – You will be asked to make your time commitment for a defined period of time—service for a two-year term. Since you have decision-making responsibilities you have a stronger obligation to attend all meetings and do not have the luxury of volunteering your time on your personal schedule—you must volunteer time on the board's schedule.

- *Legal and fiduciary responsibility* – You will play a legal role in the governance of the organization. A community association is incorporated under State laws. The board of directors has overall responsibility for the conduct of the organization. The board members must provide specific personal commitments to the work of the board (duty of care) and the board must always act in the best interests of the association (duty of loyalty) and each individual board member cannot appear to have a "conflict of interest" (you cannot receive personal benefit from a board decision).

- *Accountability* – a key principle of the board of directors is that the board operates solely as a group—if the group (board) makes a decision then every board member is responsible for that decision. You are accountable to the membership for decision-making responsibilities and using the association's financial resources effectively. Board members may be exposed to criticism from other association members based on the board's decisions or the association's problems or performance.

These obligations are mentioned not to scare you from serving on the board of directors—they are presented to make you aware of them and help you to confirm your decision to volunteer for board service.

Based on these "responsibilities" of volunteering for board service, what compels citizens to volunteer as a board member? Most volunteers suggest that the prime motivation for board service tends to be that it is an excellent way to have a substantial, and ongoing, impact in your community. As a member of a dedicated team of volunteers, you can establish long-term goals, collaborate on realizing those goals, and implement programs for improving the day-to-day quality of life of the residents and support the financial investment of the homeowners.

In addition, serving on your board provides you with a way to meet other, similar-minded owners in your neighborhood. You can build new social ties and share your passion for achieving the mission of your community association.

Volunteering for board service with your community association does bring a number of additional personal responsibilities. But those responsibilities are there because you can actually make a difference in this role. This book was written to help you to prepare for the role and help you to achieve your goals in the role of an effective community leader.

CHAPTER 3

Associations Should be Volunteer-Friendly

Community associations are resource constrained—they have limited amounts of people, time and money. As a result, the use of volunteers provides a number of advantages:

- Volunteers save the association money
- Volunteers bring needed skills
- Volunteers bring renewed energy and excitement

Based on these advantages of using volunteers, it is important that community associations need to create a "volunteer friendly" environment.

- *Make it easy to get involved and recognize achievement.* Homeowners should have an opportunity to volunteer on small programs, special events, committees or projects in order to gain an understanding of how the association works and the benefit of meeting neighbors and achieving results. And when a person does volunteer in association events, please recognize them at the next community meeting or with a personal note thanking them for their time.

- *Mentoring.* Current board members should welcome new volunteers and provide an orientation to the basics of community associations. Many times experienced board members use terms and processes that are not known by inexperienced new board members and it leaves the new members feeling left out and feeling ineffective.

- *Do not waste other volunteer's time and do not allow other volunteers to waste your time.* Do your homework. Go to meetings and events prepared. Board meetings are designed for board members to make decisions. Clarify as many questions as possible before the meeting starts. At the meetings, state your views on a subject succinctly, take a vote and move on to the next subject. If a topic needs more review, table the issue and move on.

- *Do not encourage nor practice "long-term" volunteering.* There are many examples of individual Homeowners serving on a community association Board of Directors for 5, 10 or even 20 years. I have never seen any "real" value derived from a person staying on a Board too long—but it can produce negative effects.

If a person stays on a Board for an extended period of time, the decisions effectively take on the opinion of "one person," not the collective majority of the current board. New volunteers often defer to the more experienced volunteer and do not contribute new ideas. It is the responsibility of a majority of the board members to ensure that one board member does not dominate the board.

Good associations are not built on the personality of one individual. Successful community associations establish guiding principles, good business processes, and encourage all homeowners to participate. The constant flow of new volunteers, using established management tools and practices, produces the best results for all homeowners.

CHAPTER 4

How to Make Your Volunteer Time Effective

Do you just want to volunteer your time or do you want to feel good about what you have accomplished?

I have worked with many HOA volunteers and once they start volunteering they instantly develop "ownership" in the work they do for the association. When I first joined my board, I designed some building signs for our condominium building. Now, after ten years, I still smile each time I see one of those No Parking signs. I feel "invested" in my community.

How can you make your volunteer time effective?

Practice the following concepts:

Understand your role. Read the documents that help define the role—governing documents, policies, resolutions, financial reports, meeting minutes, etc.

Know why you are volunteering. Write down the reason(s) you are joining the board of directors. This can change over time as you learn more, but focus on the reason you joined in the first place and keep reminding yourself about that objective.

Set measurable objectives. Set some measurable objectives for your time on the Board—are there two or three things that you want to see improved within the time period that you have committed to volunteering with your community association?

Manage your time. Make yourself more effective on how you spend your time and, more importantly, do not let other people waste your time. Identify time wasters in your volunteer effort. Everyone should show up for meetings on time. Everyone should do their homework and come to meetings prepared—ready to make decisions. The main purpose of board meetings is to make decisions—not spend 3 hours gossiping.

Control your personal emotions. Personal emotions will complicate decision-making by the board. You need to make decisions for the "greater good" of all of the homeowners. Do not get involved in "one on one" emotional issues—however, it is good to be emotional about the "common good" of all of the Homeowners.

Common good is defined as certain general conditions that benefit everyone. Your personal opinion is important as long as it benefits the common good of the homeowners. Set up the systems, relationships and the environment in a manner that they benefit all homeowners.

It is lonely at the top, especially when the board has a big decision to make. When bad decisions are made—most of the time, emotions are to blame. Whether it's a personal choice or a strategic business decision, emotions often crowd out objectivity. Effective leaders cannot allow emotions to overrule objectivity and sound judgment.

CHAPTER 5

How to Use this Book

This book is not a reference book. This book does not have answers for every issue that comes before a community association board of directors. That would require a very, big book!

This book is designed to give new board member volunteers a short, simple view of how you can make your time as a volunteer valuable to both you and to your community. Use this book as your "personal strategy." It is short and designed to be read in a short period of time.

It presents a new volunteer with a plan and a way to work that plan. It provides you with a framework for volunteering that allows you to use your personal skills, personal emotions and personal goals in a way that increases the odds that you will be satisfied with your time invested in your community association.

It also shows new board members some of the obstacles to making your community successful. We will try to identify some of these bad habits and show you how to combat them or stop them from occurring.

This book helps to build a foundation of knowledge that allows you to feel comfortable in the role of a board member. It is "Community Board Service 101" for homeowner associations. By following the concepts in this book, you can finish your time on the board by saying, "Look—we did that!"

CHAPTER 6

What Are Homeowner Associations?

Ignorance, on the part of the homeowners, about the role of a community association is the single biggest challenge that a board member will face.

Many "first-time" homeowners have no experience in living in a community association. The average homeowner who buys a home in a community association typically does not read the association governing documents and is not educated on the role of the community association.

Due to this lack of knowledge in association responsibilities, a high priority for you, as a volunteer board member, is to gain the knowledge and to educate your fellow homeowners on how your association works and how it can provide for a better quality of life and a more sound financial investment for all of the homeowners.

Homeowners Association Background

A homeowners association is known by a number of different names. It can be referred to as a HOA, a property owners association, a townhome association, a condominium association, or a common interest development. Even though each of these entities can be physically very different, all of them are legally structured and operate in a similar manner.

Community associations are formal organizations chartered under the laws of the State in which they exist as a nonprofit corporation.

Community associations are typically formed by a real estate developer for the purpose of marketing, managing and selling homes or lots in a residential subdivision. There are two primary attractions to packaging a group of homes together in an association:

- *Common Property and Amenities.* Developers of community associations are able to design and build common facilities and attractive amenities that can be shared between all of the homeowners, such as, swimming pools, walking trails, tennis courts, access control gates, and many others. The cost of building, operating and maintaining these structures, amenities and common property can be shared by all of the homeowners.

- *Local Control.* The developer of a community association typically has initial legal control over the association and its assets and then transfers control of the association to the Homeowners after selling off a predetermined number of units or lots. At that time, the homeowners have legal and operational control over their association.

People choose to live in community associations for numerous reasons. Many association owners value the inherent benefits offered by community association living. Community associations are designed to:

- Create a neighborhood of similarly designed and built homes that have attractive amenities that are shared by homeowners.

- Require every homeowner in the association to be a member—it is mandatory and rules and regulations apply to everyone.

- Create formal legal communities to maintain the common areas of the neighborhood and have the formal legal authority to enforce deed restrictions.

- Establish a set of guidelines, or covenants, for the proper maintenance of every residence. Covenants are issued to each homeowner in order to maintain the quality and value of homes in the community.

- Develop a sense of community for all homeowners through involvement in social functions, use of the amenities, and cooperating to achieve the common good.

How Did Homeowner Associations Get Started?

The Federal government played a big part in encouraging the development and growth of community associations in the country. In the 1960's the Federal Housing Authority authorized federal home mortgage insurance for condominiums or for houses in subdivisions, which spurred creation of associations in the suburban areas of the country. The Federal highways programs also encouraged developments near existing highways in suburban areas.

Over the next ten years, the rising costs of suburban land caused developers to increase the density of homes on the available land. To keep an attractive look to the community they clustered homes around green, open areas that were maintained by the association. These associations began providing services that formerly had been provided by local towns or municipalities funded by property taxes. As a result, local governments began promoting development of community associations as a means of improving their cash flow— more property taxes and fewer municipal services.

In the 1970's the Clean Water Act required all new real estate developments to detain storm water so that the flow to adjoining properties was no greater than the pre-development runoff. It required that all developments construct detention or retention areas to hold excess storm water until it could be released at normal flow levels. It was determined that these areas be designated as "common areas" of the community association so the responsibility to maintain them rests with the association and not local government.

Since those early years, community associations of all types and sizes have dominated the expansion of American home development. According to studies, approximately 25% of all homes in this country are in an association for a total of over 300,000 associations with more than 60 million residents.

How Are Associations Doing?

In a recent national survey, over 90% of homeowner association residents rated their experience as positive. In addition, homeowners valued the return they got for their association assessments and they believed that their association rules did indeed protect their property values.

Not too bad!

CHAPTER 7

Does the Quality of Your Association Affect the Value of Your Home?

Why should you, as a homeowner, be concerned with your homeowners association?

There are two primary drivers for homeowners to be actively interested in the quality of their community association—their financial and their social investments.

Financial Investment

The level of importance that your association has on your quality of life and your home investment is directly tied to the amount of common elements in the association—the more common elements, or common property, owned by a community association, the more impact it has on the value of your home.

First, if you live in a rural community with 50 single-family homes and only a playground for amenities, the quality of your homeowners association will have very little impact on your quality of life or your ability to sell your home in the future, since the association has very little common property.

Second, if you live in a 30-story high-rise condominium in midtown with 24-hour concierge service then the quality of your community association will have significant impact on some important issues— your quality of life, the value of your home and your ability to sell your home.

These two examples are the extremes—most associations are somewhere between each case.

As a homeowner or a board member you should know what "common elements" your association is responsible for repairing, replacing and maintaining and what services the association is expected to provide. Townhomes, condominiums and high-rise buildings all have significant levels of common elements—possibly millions of dollars.

Your total financial investment in your home can be at risk if your community association is not effectively maintaining the common elements.

Social Investment

In addition to the pure financial responsibilities of a homeowners association, a second element of value is your association's "sense of community." A sense of community refers to the interaction that a person has with others in their community and the community as a whole. It describes the level of interaction between community members—neighborhoods that have a high sense of community are likely to have ties between individuals in the neighborhood—both with personal interaction and a shared level of interest in the community. Those bonds between homeowners are typically strengthened when neighbors work together for a common cause in their community.

Your social investment in your community association is often reflected in your quality of life—"do I enjoy where I live?"

The sense of community in your neighborhood can be at risk if your association is not effectively bringing people together for the common good.

Get Involved

The answer to the original question asked at the beginning of this chapter is, "yes," your community association can have a significant impact on the value of your home. You will need to be involved.

CHAPTER 8

What Makes an Effective Homeowners Association?

"If you don't know where you are going, any road will get you there!" – Lewis Carroll, *Through the Looking Glass / Alice in Wonderland*

Leadership is a process of social influence, which maximizes the efforts of others, towards the achievement of a goal.

A community association board of directors can only be effective if they are good leaders and have a clear vision of what they want to achieve. Many times, under-performing associations suffer from "short-term thinking." My definition of short-term thinking is "the absence of long-term planning."

It is the role of the board of directors to provide the homeowners with a vision of how a successful community operates and governs effectively.

The vision must be focused and understandable because new volunteer board members have limited time to learn their destination before they start making key decisions that ensures that your "train is on the right track" to becoming a successful community.

In order to have a vision of your future community association, board members need to know what attributes make up a successful association.

Community association success factors are not dependent on the size or type of a community—whether an association is made up of single-family homes, condominiums or townhomes. The success factors relate to how the homeowners interact with each other and manage the assets of their association.

A community is made up of many home units and individual homeowners who have their own opinions and who make numerous small decisions on a daily basis. Those small decisions have the cumulative impact of selecting the track to success or failure. Boards of directors of a community play a major role in leading those homeowners and influencing them to practice good community habits or to get homeowners to correct bad habits.

The board members need to know how successful community associations operate and incorporate those "best practices" into their vision, their planning and decision-making to provide the tools to build a better community association.

Can you imagine what would happen to a community if each time a new Board of Directors was elected the decisions on every issue would change with each new personality and each new set of personal emotions?

A Foundation for a Better Community Association

There are three primary objectives for successful community associations.

- *Quality of Life (Do I enjoy where I live?)* - On a day-to-day basis the association should operate and maintain the community in a manner consistent with the expectations of a majority of the homeowners.

- *Maintain Property Values (Is my home a good Investment?)* - On a long-term basis the association should operate and maintain the community in a consistent manner that enhances the financial value of the community and its common assets.

- *Financial Integrity (Are we controlling costs?)* – The association should meet all of its financial obligations, receive good value from its expenditures and build financial funds for long-term maintenance requirements and emergencies.

Successful community associations consistently exhibit traits that allow them to be successful in having financial integrity, maintaining property values and providing a good quality of life. There are five consistent traits that establish a "benchmark" for effective community associations. Those traits are:

- A homeowners' shared vision
- A business approach to operating the association
- Effective financial planning and practices
- Effective property maintenance planning and practices
- A sense of community

CHAPTER 9

Homeowners' Shared Vision

What is a shared vision and why do you want one?

Communities that have a homeowners' shared vision are ones where a majority of homeowners agree on a vision of how they want their community to look and to operate. In one sense, this is obvious because each homeowner bought a home in the community because "they all liked what they saw when they bought their home."

The homeowners in an association start out with a shared vision. But that vision needs to be continuously reinforced and improved. If the leaders of the association are able to "paint a picture" of what the community offers and how it can be improved, the homeowners will support that vision and provide funds to continually making it better.

"This is what we liked about our community when we bought our home and this is what we want our community to be—let's work together to maintain it and make it better!"

The typical traits of communities with a shared vision include,

- The location of a community is many times the most important element in buying a home. Examples of shared vision could include the following.
    o It is in a convenient location to my work.
    o It is close to good schools.

- ° It is close to stores and shopping.
- We can afford to live here. The homes are in our price range. The annual assessments are reasonable.
- Homeowners care. A majority of the residents maintain their homes consistent with the shared vision. Everyone has similar values.
- The community leaders maintain the common areas consistent with the homeowners home maintenance. For example, the association may have a recycling program and promote "green initiatives."
- The association has amenities and social activities that are consistent with the homeowner lifestyles.
- Ongoing leadership that makes decisions and manages the association in a way that realizes the other factors of a shared vision.

Having a shared vision is important because it provides the basis for effective decision-making. If we value the same things in a home and community and have the same vision in our planning then we can probably agree on which train track to take to get there. The board of directors can make decisions that consistently keep the community on track to meet the common view of the homeowners. The homeowners, in turn, will support those decisions and contribute the funds required to maintain or improve those issues that promote the shared vision.

Homeowners must hold board members accountable. A shared vision must include an understanding by the homeowners that everyone who serves in a volunteer position with the community is accountable for operating the association in a professional manner. If your association does not have good leadership, you can blame it on the homeowners—they elected the board members.

CHAPTER 10

A Business Approach

A community association is a business.

It is incorporated under the State laws as a nonprofit corporation. Membership is automatic—you are a member of the corporation when you buy your home. You make a substantial investment in your home—you are a "shareholder" in the business of the community association. You should expect the association to use established business practices to operate the community.

The actions of the board of directors can establish the "business approach" to managing the association. A community association is limited in its resources—not enough time, people or money. The board members must work in an effective manner to leverage those limited resources to produce the best results for the homeowners' investment. Remember—you cannot afford to waste resources—they are too precious!

You can use the following community traits to determine if the association is being run like a good business:

- The board is respected by the homeowners—decision-making is transparent to homeowners and decisions are made for the total community's best interest and they do not show favoritism.
- The board understands the governing documents, establishes practical policies and makes consistent decisions.

- The board consults with industry professionals, when necessary, including property management companies, attorneys, accountants, insurance agents and engineers.

- The board knows how to reach consensus and "speaks with one voice" and makes consistent decisions.

- The board is financially responsible and uses effective financial systems and planning.

- The board maintains the common property effectively and implements a long-term preventive maintenance program.

- Board policies and rules are developed, documented and effectively communicated to all residents.

The homeowners of a community association should not accept anything less than effective business practices from its board of directors.

CHAPTER 11

Effective Financial Planning and Practices

The financial integrity of a community association is the "lifeblood" of the association. A large number of associations lack the financial resources to maintain their community and, as a result, the quality of life and the home investment value in those communities suffers.

I had a condominium association client that had a cataclysmic problem confront them in their fourth year of operation. Their parking deck developed a major structural failure. The repair would cost them $5,000,000! That calamity would have destroyed most associations.

This association had excellent board leadership and strong support from their management company and attorney. They pulled the owners together and showed them how they could overcome this significant problem. Everyone pulled together—they had a plan.

They fixed the construction defect and ten years later, the bank loan was paid off and the association had $1,000,000 in the bank! This is an extreme case, but it shows what can be accomplished when leadership develops a financial plan and gets full support from the homeowners.

Understanding the Financial Responsibilities of an Association

Board members should ask the following financial questions when they join the Board of Directors.

Key financial questions:

1. *What are the responsibilities of the association?* Good associations know what properties and assets it owns and what it is responsible for operating and maintaining based on the governing documents, good business practices and homeowner expectations.

2. *How much do those responsibilities cost?* Good associations know how much money it takes to operate the association effectively for a year. Do you know how much money it takes to effectively operate the association for the year? For each month? How much money has been required in the past years?

3. *Do we have good financial systems and controls?* Good associations have effective financial processes and reports that provide continuous monitoring of the actual financial status of the association versus the association's financial plans.

4. *Are all homeowners paying their share?* Good associations have over 90% of their homeowners paying their assessments on a timely basis. If not, then your association needs a well-defined collection process that aggressively collects assessments.

5. *Do we have an emergency fund?* Good associations have additional money set aside (approximately 2 months of revenue) in case of emergencies.

6. *Do we have a long-term financial plan?* Good associations know how much money they need to save to make repairs and replacements of major equipment and facilities over the next 20-30 years. Good associations have effective financial plans including reserve studies and annual budgets.

7. *Are we saving enough for future major repairs?* Good associations have a long-term financial plan and are actively saving enough money each year and accumulating sufficient

reserve savings to pay for repairs and replacement of major equipment and facilities when required over the next 20-year period of time.

If you do not have good answers to the questions above then you can find answers from the following sources:

- Consulting with a qualified property management company who knows effective accounting processes and systems.

- Hiring an engineer to develop a Reserve Study for your Association to tell you what you own and how much it costs to replace.

- Developing an effective annual budget for the association that identifies historical costs of operating the association and plans on future expenses.

Homeowner Funding

As a Board member, you should seek answers to the financial questions listed above. However, there is an overarching financial principle that every association must address. Effectively, all of the financial resources for the operation of a community association come directly from one primary source--the assessments paid by the homeowners. The homeowners are the single source of financial support. It is vitally important that the homeowners trust their leadership.

Many homeowner associations are dominated by "procrastinators." They tend to "put off" long-term decision-making and do not save money that should be used for properly maintaining their amenities, facilities and property. Many times homeowners do not want to pay money today for long-term maintenance.

Homeowners typically rationalize that they must minimize their association assessments because,

- "I need all of my current income now for current needs."
- "Maybe I won't live in this community when the major repairs need to be done, so I have saved that money—let somebody else pay for it when it breaks."

A majority of homeowners do not understand the responsibilities and financial obligations of a community association. As a result, they will be inclined to limit the amount of money they are willing to pay to the association. In many cases, boards refuse to increase homeowner assessments over a long period of time even though the maintenance costs are increasing every year.

The board must communicate with, and educate the homeowners on the financial responsibilities—and the possibilities--of the association if they want to maintain or build a successful community.

The homeowners must know and understand the size and scope of the financial requirements of operating and maintaining their association. If a board of directors does a good job defining the role of the association and the homeowner value that can be maintained and created then the homeowners will be willing to pay the assessments.

CHAPTER 12

Effective Property Maintenance Planning and Practices

If you, personally, are short on cash, do you normally change the oil in your car, or do you put it off for a few weeks?

There are many times when HOA's suffer from a lack of money. In many of those cases the boards of directors choose to save money by deferring maintenance on their buildings, amenities and equipment.

In effect, "they kick the can down the road!" The major problem with this type of action is that associations think they can defer maintenance continuously—year after year!

That may save the association some money in the short-term, however, in the long-term the risks of deferred maintenance tend to make the eventual costs higher than the original maintenance costs or the association risks the possibility of the equipment breaking down and the repairs costing much more to the association.

Many homeowners do not understand why they should contribute money today through higher assessments for long-term facility maintenance that in some cases is 20 years in the future—for example, major roof repairs need to be performed every 20 years.

Long-term property maintenance is a difficult concept for homeowners to understand.

Many homeowners believe that if a major piece of equipment needs to be repaired or replaced, the association should wait until it breaks down and let the homeowners at that time pay for it. (Hoping that they won't be living in the community at that time.)

Effective property maintenance programs are a major test of community leadership. Good leaders think and plan for the long-term. Preventive maintenance programs and planned long-term equipment replacement are the best uses of the association's limited monies. But it requires disciplined leadership to develop a plan and stick to it!

The benefits of effective property maintenance planning and practices include,

- *Preserves the homeowners' investment.* Preventive maintenance can extend the useful life of building components, sustaining and enhancing the common property's value.
- *Helps buildings and amenities function as they were intended and operate at peak efficiency.* Because preventive maintenance keeps equipment functioning as designed, it reduces inefficiencies in operations and energy usage.
- *Provides cost effective maintenance.* Preventive maintenance can prevent minor problems from escalating into major failures and costly repairs.
- *Sustains a safe and healthy environment.* Protecting the physical integrity of building components preserves a safe environment for residents.

Development and management of an effective maintenance plan and good practices will provide a clear direction to the board on how to repair buildings and other property consistent with a current reserve study schedule. The equipment and components will enjoy their maximum useful lives and related repair costs will be kept to a minimum. This is how a successful homeowners association was meant to operate.

A checklist on maintenance programs includes:

1. A documented inventory of all of its property, facilities and equipment. (A reserve study provides this inventory.)

2. A preventive maintenance program for all inventoried equipment.

3. The association should have a "seasonal maintenance" program for landscaping requirements for summer and winter plantings and cold weather equipment maintenance.

4. The association should have a current reserve study and use it to monitor scheduled repair or replacement with an annual physical inspection. (Reserve studies should be updated every 5 years.)

CHAPTER 13

A Sense of Community

The fifth element of operating a successful community association reflects the attitude of people who live there.

"A sense of community" is a phrase used to describe the level of interaction between neighbors, the level of participation in the association activities, and the interest of homeowners in association issues and challenges.

The operating areas that display this trait are:

- The association proactively communicates with the homeowners through newsletters, email blasts, websites and community meetings.

- Homeowners have easy access to association business information including their personal account information, board meeting minutes, financial information and more.

- The association informs and educates the homeowners on association issues.

- The association sponsors and promotes social activities for the homeowners and effective use of all of the amenities.

- Homeowners feel a sense of interest and responsibility to participate in association activities and abiding by the rules and community standards.

- Homeowners are interested in serving the community by volunteering for committee work and serving on the board of directors.

- The result: *Homeowners become good neighbors.*

The level of a sense of community will vary with each homeowners association. Successful associations incorporate ongoing programs of educating and communicating with homeowners on a continuing basis.

Homeowner Turnover

It is very important to note that many long-term residents of a community assume that since the rules have been in place for many years then every homeowner knows them. That is a popular misconception.

> *IMPORTANT. In most communities, approximately 10 - 15% of the homes are sold each year! This produces a continuous stream of new homeowners each year.*

Producing a homeowners' manual or a new owners' orientation will help significantly in assisting new homeowners in learning about the association and how they can enjoy living in their new community. Ongoing communication is key to keeping the sense of community vibrant.

CHAPTER 14

Where Do They Go Wrong?

"If your community association is working properly—it is not the most important priority in your life. However, if your community association is dysfunctional—it can be very important to your personal happiness and your financial well-being."

I believe that it takes 5-10 years for a new association to establish a "personality" or develop its community culture. It is important for the association to use that time wisely to create a foundation for operating an effective and successful community association.

If that time is not put to good use, then the community association can suffer from poor processes, ineffective systems, financial mismanagement and apathetic homeowners, who just "don't care." In addition, communities with no solid foundation can "bounce around" every two years based on different "personalities" serving on the board of directors. If there is no stability or consistency in community leadership, it can produce confused and disappointed homeowners.

Here are the primary issues that go wrong for community associations.

A Poor Foundation – When a developer turns control of a community association over to the homeowners there is typically no business structure in place. There are no systems, processes and experienced management to operate the business of the association on a day-to-day basis. The new board of directors inherits the authority and responsibility of operating a homeowners association with no experienced personnel, no checking account, little or no money in the bank, and no vendors to maintain the property. If the board does not do an effective job of putting the staff, the services, the accounting and recordkeeping systems in place, then the association is starting off in a "huge hole" that may take a long time to "crawl out of."

Apathetic Homeowners – Apathy is defined as a lack of interest or concern. Unless there is an issue that directly impacts all of the homeowners, (such as, new parking rules or special assessments) most homeowners are content knowing that someone else is handling all of the work while they enjoy the benefits of living in a managed community.

This problem is made worse when apathetic homeowners do not read their association governing documents, nor the architectural guidelines, nor the rules and regulations. If they receive a violation letter or fine then they are very likely to get angry because they do not understand what they did wrong. Homeowner apathy is a common contributor to disruptive community relationships.

Politically Driven Board Members – In the absence of experienced management and good business systems, there are many times when individual homeowners get elected to the board and put themselves in a position to "take the reins of power" and use their personal agendas to operate the community association "behind closed doors" with a total lack of transparency.

In some cases, board members may not care about the governing documents and set their personal priorities as rules and regulations. Unfortunately, if this happens to an association, the apathetic homeowners do not want to confront the "bully" as he/she destroys their community. This is another good reason why individuals should not be elected to more than two (2) terms to the board of directors.

Constantly Deferring Maintenance – Many ineffective community associations do not maintain their common property, equipment, amenities or facilities. In an effort to keep homeowner assessments low, boards often ignore the responsibility of budgeting monies for preventive maintenance programs. If your association is relatively new, you may find that the developer/builder kept the association dues "artificially low" to attract more new homebuyers.

Over time, equipment breaks down or amenities look worn out. At those times, the current homeowners are "stuck" with finding the money to fix the problem—in many cases, spending much more money than the cost of an effective preventive maintenance program.

Poor Financial Practices – Community associations have defined responsibilities and in many cases, those responsibilities require spending money. Many board members do not know what the association is responsible for nor what property the association owns.

Community associations typically have two major management failings in the financial practices arena: 1) poor collection of delinquent homeowner accounts, and 2) lack of long-term financial planning.

Perform a HOA Evaluation

To make your time on the HOA board of directors effective, you need to have some specific objectives to achieve during your time on the board. Use the key elements I have defined in this book to determine the strengths and weaknesses of your association.

I have included a community association evaluation form in the appendix of this book. It asks specific questions about your association based on the five major operating criteria discussed in the prior chapters.

Perform the evaluation and review the issues that you feel need to be improved with the operations of your HOA. Solving some of the weaknesses can become your goals while you are serving on the board.

Creating or Changing the Community Culture

Many communities waste the first 5-10 years of their existence by not establishing basic operating procedures. Two of the most common responsibilities that are ignored are an effective collection policy and long-term financial planning. Collection policies must be defined, communicated to homeowners and then, rigorously enforced. Long-term financial plans must be defined, communicated to homeowners and then, rigorously funded.

Ineffective communities are a result of uninformed board members just wanting to keep the annual assessments low and ignoring the needs of the common maintenance until it is too late. This lack of resources causes severe financial issues for the association and the homeowners.

Ineffective associations cannot make up for years of bad management practices quickly—it takes years to turn around a malfunctioning community association.

If your community suffers from some of the cultural issues listed above, then a cure may take a long time to put in place. Many times the homeowners in a community adapt to what everyone has been living with for many years and normally do not make the time or effort to change the status quo. That is the classic definition of "homeowner apathy."

Fortunately, there is an effective cure for homeowner apathy. It is called "leadership." We will identify the steps you can take to improve the culture and operations of your community. If your association has performed well in the past, these same steps can help you to effectively maintain the healthy culture of your community.

"A journey of a thousand miles begins with a single step!" – Lao-tzu –
Chinese Philosopher

CHAPTER 15

What Makes an Effective Board of Directors?

To this point, we have identified the elements that make an effective community association:

- A homeowners' shared vision
- A business approach for managing the association
- Effective financial planning and practices
- Effective property maintenance planning and practices
- A sense of community

Now we will deal with how to be an effective board of directors and how the board can establish a strategy to achieve those objectives listed above.

The Foundation for an Effective Board of Directors

Successful community associations have developed their own "culture." Organizational culture refers to culture in any type of organization, including a school, university, non-profit groups or business entities. It refers to a group or community that shares common experiences that shape the way its members understand the organization. This type of culture can be altered depending on leadership and members. This perspective believes in a culture where a majority of members buy into it.

There are critical elements that create a good foundation for a board of directors to be successful. Effective boards of directors are good at incorporating these standards into the way they work and the way they make decisions. These elements establish a community culture that produces both value for the homeowners and, consistency in the way the board of directors operates.

Effective community cultures are created by using the following critical elements:

- *Align your association with industry professionals* - Seek advice from, and hire, community association industry professionals.

- *Implement organizational structure and business best practices* – Define and document roles, rules, systems and processes for operating your association.

- *Establish a set of guiding principles for making decisions* – Create a positive strategy for decision-making that overcomes negative stereotypes and prioritizes value for all homeowners.

- *Communicate with and educate homeowners* – Continuously educate new homeowners and be transparent with association issues.

Boards of directors of community associations can be effective if they establish these elements as a foundation for their organization and they are used to establish long-term benefits and consistency in how the community association builds value for all of the homeowners. The following chapters show you how.

CHAPTER 16

Align with Industry Professionals

"Community associations are led by boards of directors made up of inexperienced volunteers who are constantly changing every few years."

Boards of directors of community associations are constantly making decisions on a myriad of issues that come before them. Many issues may seem simple "on the surface" but are not completely understood by an inexperienced volunteer.

As a committed board member, who is confronted with a question or decision about your community association, you should consistently ask yourself, "What is at risk?"

For small community associations with a few common elements and low financial requirements the "at risk" issues may not be substantial.

For larger community associations with hundreds of members, extensive common elements and large financial responsibilities, the risks can be financially and personally high.

Boards of directors should have easy access to advisors who have community association knowledge and can estimate the "potential risk" involved in the issues that come before the board. If the risk is of concern to the board, then the board should seek counsel from an appropriate professional.

Boards should align their HOA with experienced industry professionals. Industry professionals, with community association experience will help the board use best practices to preserve assets, maintain property values, establish continuity, and provide assistance with operational, legal or financial matters.

Board members have a "fiduciary responsibility" to the association. A fiduciary is a person who stands in a special relationship of trust and confidence with respect to his or her obligations to all of the homeowners.

One of the primary solutions to fulfilling the role of a fiduciary is to rely on experts. Being a director does not require you to know everything in trying to make the right decisions for your association. You should rely on experts who can provide an opinion on many specific issues. The duty to inquire and rely on experts is part of your prudent business judgment rule. You can reject the expert's advice for valid reasons if you choose to, but you should always seek advice when you need it.

The industry professionals typically needed by a community association include the following experts:

- *Attorney* – Every association must have access to an attorney who is knowledgeable about community association operations and legal issues.

- *Insurance Agent* – Every association must have access to an insurance agent experienced in community associations.

- *Accountant* – Many small, self-managed community associations do not use professional accounting services and may have qualified individuals living in the community who are capable of "keeping the books" for a small association, but every HOA needs access to accounting skills in the industry.

- *Engineer* – Engineers are typically needed by larger community associations that have substantial facilities or common elements that could include items like, retention ponds, buildings, townhomes or condominiums or other structures and mechanical systems.

- *Property Management Services* – The advantage of property management service companies are that they give an association access to individuals with community association expertise and accounting knowledge and effective accounting systems.

- *Community Association Manager* – Larger community associations should align with a property management service company that includes an assigned community association manager. The manager can act as a "constant" industry advisor to the board of directors relative to industry practices and many of the typical exposures for the association and the board members.

Professionals Add Consistency

The use of industry professionals by a community association will also provide a substantial advantage for the long-term benefit of the association—consistency in decision-making over a long period of time. That consistency will establish "community standards" that will be well known to all of the homeowners and provide a constant use of "industry best practices" by the association in it's organizational, financial and legal dealings.

CHAPTER 17

Establish Organizational Structure and Business Best Practices

The process of implementing organizational structure and industry best practices is made up of a number of key components. The key components are like the pieces of a jigsaw puzzle—the more pieces you have put together, the clearer the picture is that you are trying to create. If you have all of the pieces put together than everyone involved can see the picture and understand their role in the organization. Part of your strategy is to add more pieces of the puzzle to provide more tools for your board to use to make the picture clear.

A board of directors can create structure and processes by developing and using the following "best practices puzzle pieces":

- *Governing Documents* - Understanding and applying the governing documents.

- *Book of Resolutions* - Creating a Book of Resolutions to establish rules, regulations and policies on homeowner guidelines and board administrative processes.

- *Homeowners Manual* – Creating a basic manual to educate homeowners on essential rules, regulations and the governing documents.

- *Reserve Study* - Maintaining and following a current Reserve Study for funding needed for replacement and maintenance of the association's property.

- *Community Strategic Plan* – Develop and update a long-term community plan for maintaining and improving the association.

- *Annual Budget* – Develop a realistic annual budget for the association that addresses all of the responsibilities of the homeowners and meets their expectations.

Developing these components and using them effectively will provide the association with community standards that will provide organizational structure for long-term consistency and incorporate industry best practices into your homeowners association. We will review each of these components or "puzzle pieces" in the next few chapters.

CHAPTER 18

Best Practice – Understanding the Governing Documents

The typical homeowner in a community association does not read nor understand the association's governing documents.

What are the Governing Documents?

Governing documents are a set of legal documents that govern the relationship between homeowners and the community association. They typically include, articles of incorporation, the declaration or covenants, maps, bylaws, resolutions, rules and regulations. This collection of documents creates the legal structure and operation of the community. The goals of the governing documents are intended to preserve and enhance property values, protect the owners and the community and to promote harmonious living.

The governing documents also establish a number of the financial responsibilities of the community association. If the association is responsible for maintaining the landscaping, or the swimming pool, or the roofs of all of the units, then those responsibilities must be included in the association's annual budget.

Reading the governing documents before you take a seat on the board of directors is a good idea and it will help you understand the scope of the documents and what issues they impact. However, reviewing the governing documents "after" a few months on the board can also be eye opening. You will realize that a number of the association's ongoing issues are actually dealt with in the documents and the problems can be resolved by following the directions in the governing documents. Even if you have looked through the governing documents, take a second look after a couple of months on the board—you will find answers to a number of association issues.

The declaration and the bylaws contain a number of key elements that should be understood by the homeowners.

The Declaration

The declaration, also referred to as the covenants or CCR's (Covenants, Conditions & Restrictions), primarily deals with the rights of ownership. In the absence of any restrictions, the landowner typically has full rights to do what they want to do with the land and those rights are spelled out in the deed that is recorded in the county land records. If there are provisions which limit the rights of ownership then these are referred to as deed restrictions or covenants. These covenants "run with the land." That means that they apply to the property, no matter who owns it or how many times it is sold.

Instead of inserting all of the same covenants and restrictions into each deed, the developer creates the Declaration of Covenants and records those covenants for all of the property owned in the community association. Those terms are binding on all of the property and its owners and every succeeding owner.

Now you see why it is important for every owner and board member to read and understand the provisions of the declaration/covenants.

A declaration,

- Defines the areas owned by each owner and those owned by the association.
- Creates the legal relationship between all of the owners and to the association for the purpose of maintaining, governing and funding the organization.

- Establishes the protective standards, the restrictions and the obligations on those areas including prohibitions and architectural standards.

- In addition to the bylaws, it creates the administrative structure for the operation and management of the association.

The Bylaws

Bylaws are the formal governing regulations for the administration and management of a community association as an organization— the roles of the Board members, requirements for board meetings, notices to homeowners, election of board members, and similar governing processes.

Read and Understand the Governing Documents

Each community association is unique and each set of governing documents is unique. It is very important that every board member read the governing documents and seek an understanding of what is contained in them and the implications to the homeowners and board of directors.

CHAPTER 19

Best Practice – Book of Resolutions

What would happen to your association if each time a new board member was elected the rules and regulations would change?

Policies and Resolutions Built on Industry Best Practices

A key to successful community associations is the creation of written policies that "interpret" the legal governing documents into everyday language—understandable by all of the homeowners.

Resolutions are the puzzle pieces that associations use to establish policies and rules and to provide the board of directors with effective "tools" for interpreting and applying the governing document covenants and guidelines in a more practical form that can be learned and understood by community residents.

Policies and rules are a practical way of defining the "standards" of the community association. Many times the governing documents are not clear nor do they fully define the actions that will be taken under a set of circumstances. Policies, by design, are flexible and can be customized to make them much easier to implement and administer than amending the governing documents, which can be difficult and expensive.

A good example of how rules and policies can provide a more practical method of explaining the governing documents is how associations explain the use of the swimming pool.

For example, the governing documents may state the following: "owners, their family members, guests, tenants, invitees, or agents my use the swimming pool."

The board can adopt a resolution to create a rule that gives a more clear understanding by stating: "An owner is allowed no more than five (5) guests at the swimming pool at one time. Pool hours are limited to 7:00 am to 10:00 pm daily." This is the type of direct language that can be used to communicate to all homeowners.

The most common approach to clarifying and applying the governing documents—is to adopt resolutions to create policies and rules.

Resolutions are legal documents that are developed, adopted and voted on by the board of directors to formalize specific association procedures, prohibitions or remedies. Resolutions are the preferred method of establishing operating procedures and association rules for the association and typically deal with policy and administrative issues. Resolutions are enacted by a vote of the Board of Directors and do not require membership votes. Typically, resolutions should be recorded with the local county authorities to be made part of the association's governing documents.

Policies are informal statements that define a plan of action or a strategy to guide board decisions or to communicate required behaviors to homeowners. Typical examples of policies include, a move-in and move-out policy, a reserve fund investment policy, a delinquent account collection policy, a pet owner policy or vehicle towing policy.

Rules are formal regulations that govern homeowners' personal conduct, actions or procedures that serve the best interests of the community. Rules are typically created by resolutions. Rules would include areas such as, hours of operations, control of pets, parking restrictions, noise violations, etc. Any proposed rule must comply with the governing documents, as well as, state and local statutes.

Rules can come directly from the governing documents or can be defined by the board of directors. The most effective method of communicating association rules to homeowners is to create a Homeowner's Manual and provide it to every resident.

Developing a Book of Resolutions,

- Makes it easier to communicate association guidelines to homeowner.

- Provides guidelines to future boards of directors to ensure consistent decision-making over a reasonable period of time.

- Establishes written community standards.

CHAPTER 20

Best Practice – Reserve Study

Every community association is unique in size, shape and amenities. It is the responsibility of the community association to maintain, repair or replace all the physical components that are owned by and make up an association.

Careful planning for future repairs and replacements is in the best interests of the association, both physically and financially. Associations must establish a special financial fund to pay for those responsibilities. Those monies are referred to as a reserve fund and the written assessment that identifies all of the community's assets and defines the total cost of properly maintaining all of the assets is called a reserve study.

A reserve study is typically prepared by a qualified engineering company or individual. There are two components of a reserve study—a physical analysis and a financial analysis. The physical analysis consists of a listing of all of an association's common area components with the current physical status of each component, the remaining life of that asset, and the estimated time and cost of repairing or replacing each component.

The financial analysis compares the total costs of paying for all future repairs with the current level of the association's reserve fund to determine a funding plan to save sufficient monies to pay for all future repairs.

A reserve study may confuse many board members. It is a long report with a substantial number of facts, figures, tables and alternatives. It is important that a board of directors "translates" the study into a management plan to create a reserve fund to pay for all of the needed property replacements and repairs.

Also, lenders look for signs of financial health when reviewing mortgage applications. Communities with inadequate reserve funds may find themselves at risk for mortgage denials

Careful planning for the future repair and replacement of association assets is the board of directors' fiduciary responsibility and it demonstrates good stewardship of the association's money—a reserve fund is the foundation of good stewardship by every homeowner.

IMPORTANT!

Establishing and correctly funding a reserve fund is one of the most critical elements for a successful community association. Do not ignore the need for a planned reserve fund for your association.

CHAPTER 21

Best Practice – Community Strategic Plan

Many community associations suffer from a lack of long-term planning. A long-term plan does not have to be complicated. It can be as simple as wanting to build a children's playground and needing two years to save the money.

The primary objectives of a community strategic plan are to,

- Identify the current status, strengths and weaknesses of the association, based on the perspectives of homeowners, board members and local real estate agents.

- Define a future vision of the association that addresses both the weaknesses of the association and the expectations of the homeowners.

- Create a plan to implement the expectations, the costs of those expectations and the period of time it will take to financially prepare and implement the plan.

A community plan is a simple strategic plan for your association. It should be reviewed and updated every year or two.

One of the most important aspects of creating a community plan is that it establishes a "shared vision" of the community. The community strategic plan describes a picture of the future that builds a bond with the homeowners and secures their personal and financial support for the vision to be realized.

With a clear and concise strategic plan, your board and future community volunteers will enjoy a roadmap that helps them stay focused on the important tasks and goals that will provide long-term benefits to the community. Most importantly, it makes short-term decision-making much easier because boards can determine whether a current issue or challenge fits into their long-term plan.

An excellent approach to building trust between the board and the homeowners is to solicit input from owners early in the planning cycle. A couple of good methods include a community brainstorming session and a well-designed community survey. Don't forget to collect input from renters in the community. Their perspective may be different but valuable.

It may also be useful and enlightening to solicit input from real estate agents that specialize in your community. For example, a real estate agent hears the positive and negative perceptions of potential buyers in your community. The negative perceptions can be turned into a future objective for your community strategic plan.

An effective community strategic plan is an excellent tool to use to excite current homeowners about the future and solidify their financial support.

CHAPTER 22

Best Practice – Annual Budget

I have selected the annual budget as the last component needed to "complete the jigsaw puzzle" that will create an operating structure for your homeowners association. I have put it last because some or all of the other components may require funding. If they do, then those monies must be added to the annual budget if you are serious about accomplishing them.

It is critically important that your board of directors develop a realistic annual budget for your association. What do I mean by the term, "realistic annual budget?"

A realistic budget means that the board of directors understands what obligations the association is responsible for and has identified the correct amount of money needed to perform those annual commitments.

As many homeowners have discovered, when developers sell homes, condos or townhomes, they tend to "understate the annual homeowner assessments." They keep the annual fee low to sell homes and ignore many of the financial responsibilities of the homeowners association.

To further complicate the financial planning for the association, many homeowners insist that the annual assessments must stay the same every year—they do not want to see any increases.

Educate the Homeowners

The value of using the prior chapters' list of components, or puzzle pieces, to operate your homeowners association is that those same components can be used to educate the homeowners on the responsibilities of the association. The governing documents, operating polices, a reserve study and a strategic plan can be used to explain to homeowners what the money is needed for and how that will provide a better quality of life and better home investment.

CHAPTER 23

Establish and Use Association Value Principles

"A homeowners association was created to produce <u>value</u> for its homeowners."

If there is an absence of communication and information going to homeowners from their community association, there is a good chance that homeowners will form a "negative impression" of the association and its board of directors.

The last of the four major elements of effective boards of directors deals with framing the actions of the homeowners association as value-driven for the homeowners.

Homeowners can easily form negative thoughts about their associations because their only exposure with the board of directors is when they receive a letter citing them with a violation and a fine, or a letter telling them that they will have an increase in annual assessments.

Community associations should not be about "controlling and fining people"—they should be about producing value for homeowners' investments and improving their quality of life.

Boards should not promote the idea that "their role is to enforce restrictive covenants on all homeowners." Instead, board members should define their role as a positive influence to, "educate, communicate and reach decisions that achieve the homeowners expected quality of life."

Communication with homeowners should be proactive and informative.

"We would like to thank all of our neighbors who pick up after their dogs and dispose of the waste properly. Thank you!"

The first question that boards of directors should ask themselves before they make decisions on association matters is, "how can this decision provide value to our homeowners?"

As an HOA board member, perhaps the most compelling issue you will need to confront is that a majority of homeowners in your association are more influenced by "emotions" than they are by facts, figures or logic.

People tend to see things that are happening now, as more urgent than those that will happen in the future. This tendency is often referred to as "discounting the future."

Also, it is often easier to get people to agree now on a solution, if they can postpone implementation until some time in the future.

People tend to believe that they will be in a better position to change in the future; they expect to have more time, more money, and fewer demands then than they do now. While experience does not support this belief, it is one that provides people with the motivation to act in the present toward a future goal.

Consequently, it is often easier to get people to agree now on a change that won't take place until some point in the future. You will no doubt recognize this as a strategy commonly used by merchandisers—buy now, pay later!

"Discounting the future" occurs constantly with homeowners in an HOA. The most prevalent case of discounting the future occurs when money for long-term reserve funds are needed and homeowners do not want to increase their current HOA fees to fund it. Board members need to "paint a picture of the future" to encourage current homeowners to start paying for the future—today!

Talk in Terms of Future Value

Boards of directors should establish a set of guiding principles for decision-making that consistently strive to produce value for all homeowners. All decisions should be framed in the perspective of, "how will this decision produce value for the homeowners." Boards of directors should consider all of their decisions based on what end result they are trying to achieve.

If you were to listen to some of the biggest critics of homeowners associations, their primary complaint is that the association's board of directors is "controlling and restricting" the homeowners from living in and enjoying their homes. Critics complain that boards tell them what they cannot do to their own homes and impose fines on them.

To offset that negative perception, boards of directors should "frame" their actions in terms of what value each of these responsibilities produces for the greater good of all of the homeowners.

Establishing board value principles will provide decision-making consistency and continuity over a long period of time, even though there may be constant turnover in the volunteer board members.

Establish value principles and board ethics that guide the board of directors in consistent and effective decision-making. Re-think what creates negative perceptions of homeowners associations by the homeowners. Build a positive vision of the community and how certain decisions will help produce that vision. Follow the track that will produce future homeowner values.

Using value principles in decision-making will result in the following good community traits:

- Effective leadership

- Cost-effective operations
- Attractive amenities
- Good neighbors
- Knowledgeable residents

Boards Should be Committed to Value Principles

The following value principles should be reviewed, discussed and practiced by the board of directors at the beginning of every year to affirm their commitment to providing value to all of the homeowners.

Value Principle 1 – Active homeowners having a voice in their association produces "effective leadership"

Boards should continuously encourage homeowners' involvement in their HOA's. Associations that have active homeowners who attend meetings, read governing documents, hold social gatherings and hold elected board members accountable will have effective leadership.

Homeowners must participate in their government. Association leaders must work in an open forum and invite input. The decisions must be made by the board of directors but the board should reflect the will of the people.

Homeowners have the power to elect a board that will provide the best leadership.

Value Principle 2 – Good financial practices will produce "cost-effective operations"

Boards should continuously show that they are good stewards of the association's money. The board should provide a well-run community that homeowners trust and are willing to support financially—if the homeowners want it and they trust leadership, they will be willing to pay for it. Boards should consistently establish long-term financial planning, establish strong financial resolutions and policies, utilize effective financial processes and systems, and monitor financial performance with good financial reports.

Constantly show homeowners examples of effective cost-savings projects and competitive bidding.

Value Principle 3 - Good maintenance practices for the common property will produce "attractive amenities"

Maintain the common areas and amenities to reflect an attractive appearance and activities for everyone to enjoy. Remember why you bought your home in the first place—what did you like about the neighborhood and its amenities. Continue to maintain the common areas and amenities and make them better. Show homeowners photos of ongoing maintenance projects. That will attract even more interested new buyers.

Value Principle 4 - Education and enforcement of the covenants will produce "good neighbors"

Maintain the architectural design of the community to consistently meet the shared vision for homeowners to have pride in their community. A majority of the homeowners in a community establish the "community standards" for a neighborhood. They maintain their homes to a particular standard and it is reasonable to expect all of the homeowners to meet those standards. If everyone meets those expectations, they are being good neighbors.

It is not about fining and scolding homeowners—it is about keeping the community attractive.

Value Principle 5 - Communication & education will produce "knowledgeable residents"

Encourage all homeowners through meetings, newsletters and social activities, to maintain their individual homes consistent with community standards that reflect a safe and enjoyable neighborhood. You should not have people in your community who can use the excuse, "I didn't know that rule." The rules and expectations should be communicated in many ways and many times per year.

Boards of directors should stay on a track that produces value for the homeowners. And the change must be expressed in terms of the value that the homeowner will receive. Adopting and practicing the principles shown above will establish a high level of trust between the board and the homeowners.

CHAPTER 24

Educate Homeowners with Ongoing Communications

"Apathetic homeowners do not read the governing documents, nor do they read rules and regulations, nor do they attend association meetings, nor do they understand association responsibilities. As a result, they break rules that they do not even know exist."

Good community associations need to continuously educate homeowners and proactively communicate with them about association issues and solutions. A key reason for continually educating homeowners is that the rate of homeowner turnover in a community is high. According to recent surveys, the average homeowner owns their single-family home for eight (8) years. The average condominium or townhome homeowner owns their home for six (6) years. That results in over 25% new homeowners to a community every two years!

Board Transparency

Boards of directors that practice the operating standards listed above will be creating a very transparent organization. The standards and the transparency will build trust between the homeowners and the leaders of the community. Trust is the "basic building block" of an effective community association.

CHAPTER 25

Getting Things Done Together

At this stage we have discovered,

- The value of volunteers
- What is a community association
- What can go wrong
- What makes a good community association
- What makes an effective board of directors

So now, we know where we want to go, but how do we get there? How do we get on the right track and put it all together to get the results that we want? And how do you make your volunteer time for the community effective and worthwhile?

Establishing a good foundation for an effective community association is critical to its success. A large part of that foundation is the establishment of a common commitment to producing value for homeowners and the establishment of the proper tools to govern the association—the policies, a reserve study, a long-term plan, or an annual budget.

The next step is to understand the roles of all of the "players" in an association and to coordinate effective working relationships in meeting the association's objectives on a continuing basis.

The Role of the Homeowner

Remember, membership in a community association is "mandatory" for a homeowner—you have responsibilities as a member.

All homeowners should assume responsibility to protect property values and secure a lifestyle that all residents can enjoy. As a member of your community association, your legal and practical responsibilities to the community association include:

- Educating yourself on the role of your community association and its responsibilities
- Participating in community activities including voting, association meetings and social functions
- Complying with the governing documents, rules and regulations, architectural guidelines, policies and procedures, and
- Paying the annual assessment necessary to operate the community association.

The Role of the Board of Directors

As the primary group of people accountable for the governance of the association, the board of directors has several key responsibilities:

1. Represent the organization's homeowners and ensure governance transparency.

2. Articulate the organization's strategic focus and priorities, set strategic direction and develop long-term plans.

3. Provide financial stewardship and proper financial oversight.

4. Seek advice and industry standards from qualified sources, in particular, community association managers, attorneys and accountants.

5. Provide a management accountability system—delegate, advise, support, and regularly review the association manager's performance.

6. Ensure the homeowner's understanding and trust of the association and ensure legal and ethical integrity.

7. Rejuvenate the board; select and orient new board members on a regular basis; assess board performance.

The list of responsibilities above can be be summarized with one word:

"Leadership"

CHAPTER 26

Build Working Relationships and Alliances

"Relationship building is one of the most important leadership activities you can engage in. Your influence goes only as far as the quality of your relationships."

The secret to getting things done on a community association board of directors is to build alliances. Alliances are a key part of what a leader does. Alliances provide a network of trusted sources. Skilled neighborhood leaders build relationships within their community association so they do not work in a vacuum. Use the following steps to build effective alliances:

Have a purpose for engaging people. Define your purpose. For example, you want to improve the home values in the community. A strong sense of purpose provides a solid base to create an effective alliance of people. Frame your approach to others with a win-win solution—support is easier to gain when you are offering to help solve someone else's problem. It is important to have an attitude of collaboration.

Frame your ideas into a short, focused storyline. Do not ramble on and on with why your idea is a good one. Describe your objective, identify the key obstacles or issues to be overcome and ask for other ideas or solutions. Tell a brief, effective story—one that others can remember and use. You should be able to present your story in less than 2 minutes.

Continue to grow your base. Leaders should not become content with their initial effort. Alliances take consistent growth to keep the momentum. Too often we engage with only one or two supporters of our ideas. Continue to explain to other board members the ideas that you have and ask what they are trying to accomplish.

In building alliances with other board members and homeowners, remember the following relationship principles:

- Effective communication forms the base for an alliance. Tell your allies what you need and listen to what they need.

- Treat your allies as equals.

- Exhibit professionalism—alliances only work when trust is present.

- Do not form an "exclusive club" of specific personalities that the rest of the people will fear and resent.

- Be the person who is willing to do extra to strengthen the alliance.

- Keep your promises. People need to depend on you and the deadlines you commit to.

Building alliances can be a delicate process. It takes time, effort, commitment and sometimes not getting what you want. But, in a volunteer organization like a community association, if you want to make your time on the board effective, you must have allies to accomplish your objectives.

CHAPTER 27

A Board of Directors is a Team Sport

As a leader in your community, your opinion is not important—building a consensus around your opinion is important. Consensus is defined as a majority of opinion—general agreement or harmony.

Serving on a board of directors is a team sport!

Do not allow your board of directors to become "a group of individual personalities with their own personal agendas." You cannot be effective if you (or one of your associates) volunteer and spend your time and efforts on a "personal agenda."

Use the information provided in this book to give yourself a set of "talking points" to influence the board members. You want to use these best practices developed by hundreds of successful community associations as objectives that will benefit everyone.

You are not in this role alone. Over a period of time, you want everyone on the "association team" to benefit from the direction that is set, from the tools that are available, from the communication that takes place and the investments in the common property.

The board must take actions of that are collaborative and inclusive—that encourages homeowners to talk to each other so everyone understands the risks and rewards of the association's efforts.

Governance is the set of principles that allow leadership to function effectively and efficiently in a community association.

Governance – the process by which the people, involved in an organization, examine vet, and make important decisions that direct their collective efforts.

Governance is base on the following sets of principles:

Principle 1: The Board Represents the Owners. The board of a non-profit organization represents the ownership of the organization just as a business board represents its stockholders. Simply put, the board governs on behalf of persons who are not seated at the board table. The primary relationship the board of directors must maintain is its relationship with its "owners."

Principle 2: The Board Speaks with One Voice. If your board is to make authoritative decisions and lead on a given issue, then it must have a single voice. This one voice principle does not mean that there should be unanimity or lack of diversity on the board. Rarely will a vote be unanimous. Those board members who lose a vote, however, must accept that the board has spoken with the majority and that its decision must be implemented as decided.

Principle 3: A Board Should Define Goals, Policies and Rules. The function of the board is to set policy. A board of directors should focus on the goals of the association and the policies that will achieve them. The board is accountable for the way the organization conducts itself.

Win One for the Team

We have touched on a number of subjects. The intent is for you to form a foundation of understanding and a way of working that will allow you to spend your time effectively helping your homeowners association. Volunteering time and effort for a homeowners association board of directors can be a very rewarding experience. I believe that you should measure the success of your time on the board in the success achieved by the entire homeowners association. Win one for the team!

CHAPTER 28

Have Fun and Take Pride

Thank you for your service!

Appendix: Community Assessment

The objective of this community assessment is to have the board members rate the strengths and weaknesses of their association against a "benchmark" of key performance areas including finance, maintenance, residential programs, administration and board effectiveness.

Answer the following questions on a scale of 1-5, with 1 being very low and a 5 being very high. Add comments if necessary.

Community Name:

Board Member:

Date:

I. Homeowner Shared Vision

    a. Does the community have good "curb appeal". Is it attractive to the general public?

    b. Does the community have amenities that are consistent with the defined lifestyle?

    c. Does the association promote a sense of security from crime and is it perceived to be a safe neighborhood?

    d. Is the community primarily made up of owner-occupied homes and are leased homes limited by the governing documents?

    e. Do community leaders understand the homeowners' vision of the association and do they make decisions that support that vision?

II. Business Approach to Managing the Association

    a. Is the Board of Directors respected by the homeowners?

    b. Does the board operate in a business-like manner that works for the best interests of the whole community and is the decision-making process transparent to the homeowners?

    c. Does the board run their board meetings in a business-like manner and they do not waste time

    d. Does the board know and understand the governing documents and apply their decision in a consistent manner?

    e. Are the association's governing documents current, complete, well-written and effective?

    f. Are the association records and financial accounts maintained in a timely and accurate manner?

    g. Does the board enforce the rules and standards in a consistent manner for all homeowners?

    h. Does the board reach consensus and "speak with one voice" or do they all have their own opinions?

    i. Does the board adopt written policies that reflect fair community standards that can be communicated to homeowners?

    j. Is the board const-conscience and does it utilize qualified vendors at competitive costs?

    k. Does the board maintain sufficient insurance coverage on the operations of the association?

    l. Is the board open to input and regularly seeks the advice of professionals, including attorneys, community managers, accountants and engineers when necessary?

III. Effective Financial Planning & Practices

   a. Do the homeowners know and understand the scope and size of the financial obligations of the association and are they willing to pay assessments consistent with those obligations?

   b. Does the association have an effective program for collecting money from delinquent homeowners?

   c. Is the annual budget realistic and does it meet the association's expectations?

   d. Does the board use timely and accurate financial reports to manage the association's operations?

   e. Does the association have well-defined cash controls in place to protect the financial assets of the community?

   f. Does the association have a current reserve study or plan in place and is the association on plan?

   g. Does the association have adequate cash flow to pay for the normal month-to-month operating expenses?

   h. Does the association have adequate money in its reserve fund account to meet both large emergency requirements and planned replacement of its equipment?

IV. Effective Maintenance Plan and Practices

   a. Are the association's building, facilities, amenities and common property well constructed and well maintained?

   b. Is there a detailed inventory of all of the equipment, facilities, amenities and other assets owned by the association?

   c. Are all of the association's building systems and equipment covered and maintained by a preventive maintenance program?

d. Is there an effective seasonal maintenance program in place and well managed for items, such as, flower beds and the swimming pool.

e. Are major capital assets, such as, building roofs, roadways and retention ponds repaired and maintained on a timely basis?

f. Does the association actively seek competitive bids on all major capital expenditures?

V. A Sense of Community

a. Does the board proactively communicate with homeowners through newsletters, email blasts, websites or community meetings?

b. Does the association educate and inform homeowners about the rules, regulations and association issues of the community?

c. Do homeowners have easy access to association information including personal account information, board meeting minutes, financial information and more?

d. Does the association sponsor and promote social activities for the homeowners and encourage use of the amenities?

e. Is there an active interest by Homeowners wanting to volunteer for committees or to serve on the Board of Directors?

f. Do homeowners feel a sense of interest and responsibility in participating in association activities and abiding by the rules and community standards?